Learning the Cello

Book One

For individual study, single-string classes, or mixed-string classes

expanded edition

by Cassia Harvey

CHP281

C. Harvey Publications

www.charveypublications.com

Warmup Exercise for the Beginning of Class

0 1 2 3 4 3 2 1

0 1 2 3 4 3 2 1

0 1 2 3 4 3 2 1

0 1 2 3 4 3 2 1

0

Play this exercise on all four strings.
Use it as a warmup every time you play.

1. Parts of the Viola and Bow

VIOLA

1. scroll
2. peg box
3. pegs
4. nut
5. neck
6. fingerboard
7. sides
8. f holes
9. bridge
10. tailpiece
11. fine tuners

Chinrest or sponge goes here.

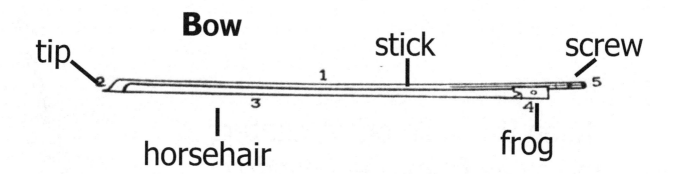

Bow

tip   stick   screw

horsehair   frog

2. Taking care of the Viola

Keep your viola away from pets.

Don't let the viola drop (or the bow).

The wood is very fragile.

No water on the viola or bow.

Keep the viola off of heaters and away from open windows.

3. Taking care of the Bow

Don't touch the bow hair!

Righty-tighty: To tighten the bow, turn the screw to the right.

Lefty-loosey: To loosen the bow, turn the screw to the left.

Always loosen the bow when you are finished playing.

Keep the viola and bow up off the floor.

4. The Open Strings

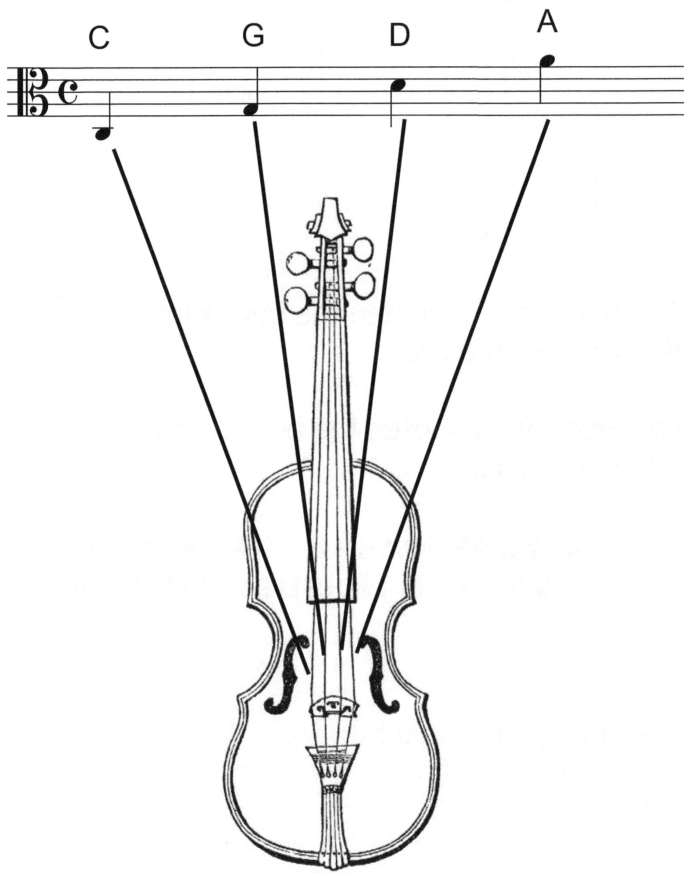

5. Pluck the Open Strings
(Lowest to Highest)

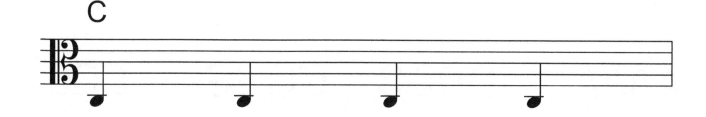

6. Open String Song

play with long bows, from the frog to the tip

CCCC GGGG DDDD AAAA

AAAA DDDD GGGG CCCC

CC GG DD AA AA DD GG
CC

CGCG GDGD DADA ADGC

7. Mississippi Hot Dog

4 short bows and 2 long bows

Play the rhythm "Mississippi Hot Dog"
on each note:

C C G G   D D A A

C G D A   A D G C

C G G D   D A A D

8. Blueberry Song:
Long-Short Short

C - CC   C - CC

G - GG   G - GG

D - DD   D - DD

A - AA   A - AA

D - DD   D - DD

G - GG   G - GG

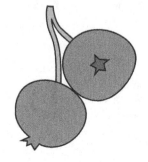

9. Speedy Open Strings

DDDD AAAA

DDDD GGGG

CCCC GGGG

DDAA DDAA

DDGG DDGG

CCGG CCGG

10. The Finger Numbers

Using the Fingers

0 is for open string
1 is for first finger
2 is for second finger
3 is for third finger
4 is for fourth finger
The thumb goes under the neck of the viola.

11. First Finger Song

0000   1111   0000   1111

00 11 00 11   1111   0000

String Class: Play
on the A string or
D string.
Solo: Can be played
on all 4 strings.

12. First Finger Challenge

0011   0011   0000   1111

0011   1100   1111   0000

0101   0000   0101   0000

13. Second Finger Song

0000   1111   2222   1111

0000   1111   2222   1111

00 11 22 11 00 11 22 11 00

String Class: Play
on the A string or
D string.
Solo: Can be played
on all 4 strings.

14. Second Finger Challenge!

11 00 11 22 11 22 1111

22 11 2121 2121 0000

15. Hot Cross Buns

210 -   210 -

0000 1111

210 -

String Class: Play
on the A string or
D string.
Solo: Can be played
on all 4 strings.

16. Au clair de la Lune

0001   2 - 1 -   0211   0 ---

0001   2 - 1 -   0211   0 ---

17. Mary Had a Little Lamb

2 1 0 1

String Class: Play
on the A string or
D string.
Solo: Can be played
on all 4 strings.

2 2 2 -

1 1 1 -

2 2 2 -

2 1 0 1

2 2 2 2

1 1 2 1

0 - - -

18. Third Finger Song

0000   1111   2222   3333

2222   3333   2222   1111

00 11 22 33 22 33 22 11 00

String Class: Play
on the A string or
D string.
Solo: Can be played
on all 4 strings.

19. Third Finger Challenge!

11 22 33 22 11 22 33 22

22 33 21 21 00 11 23 23

20. Finger Training

0 1 2 3   4 3 4 3

4 3 2 1   0 1 0 1

0 1 2 3   4 3 4 3

4 3 2 1   0 1 0 1

2 3 2 3   2 1 2 1 0

String Class: Play
on the D string.
Solo: Can be played
on all 4 strings.

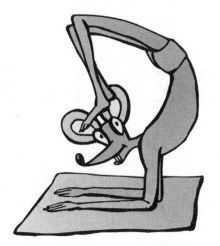

21a. Ode to Joy

If playing this in a class,
start on the D string.

Beethoven

2 2 3 4 4 3 2 1

0 0 1 2 2 1 1 -

2 2 3 4 4 3 2 1

0 0 1 2 1 0 0 -

Can you figure out
the rest?

21b. Special Challenge:
Ode to Joy, Second Part

Start on the D string.

1 1 2 0   1 2 3 2 0

1 2 3 2 1   0 1 **Play this on the G String**
1 -

2 2 3 4   4 3 2 1

0 0 1 2   1 - 0 0

22. Rests

This sign is called a quarter rest:

When you see a rest like this,
stop playing and count to 1
before playing again.

String Class: Play on the
A string or the D string.
Solo: Can be played on all
4 strings.

23. Au clair de la Lune

0   0   0   1   2   ⅔   1   ⅔

0   2   1   1   0   ⅔   ⅔   ⅔

Repeat

Breaking the notes up

Now we break the notes up with a line: |

String Class: Play on the
D string.
Solo: Can be played on all
4 strings.

24. Purcell's Rigaudon

3 3 2 1 | 0 𝄽 𝄽 𝄽

1 1 2 0 | 3 𝄽 0 𝄽

3 3 2 1 | 0 𝄽 𝄽 𝄽

1 1 2 0 | 3 𝄽 𝄽 𝄽

25. A Regal March
(on the D String if playing in a class)

0012 | 3322 | 0012 | 1100

0012 | 3322 | 0012 | 1100

26. Three-Leaf Clover
(on the D String if playing in a class)

222 | 012 | 111 | 444

222 | 012 | 111 | 000

333 | 222 | 012 | 111

333 | 222 | 121 | 000

27. Falling Down!

(on the D String if playing in a class)

2210 | 3321 | 2012 | 1 𝄾 1𝄾

2210 | 3321 | 0211 | 0 𝄾 0 𝄾

28. Waltz

(on the D String if playing in a class)

012 | 333 | 210 | 111

012 | 321 | 232 | 111

012 | 333 | 210 | 111

012 | 333 | 221 | 000

29. Reaching Saturn

(on the D String if playing in a class)

012 | 210 | 123 | 3 𝄾 𝄾

123 | 321 | 234 | 4 𝄾 𝄾

432 | 234 | 321 | 1 𝄾 𝄾

321 | 123 | 210 | 0 𝄾 𝄾

30. Back to Earth

(on the D String if playing in a class)

0210 | 1111 | 1321 | 2222

2012 | 3333 | 2312 | 0000

31. Neptune
(on the D String if playing in a class)

2212 | 3323 | 2212 | 021𝄽

2212 | 3210 | 2232 | 120𝄽

32. Flying Away
(on the D String if playing in a class)

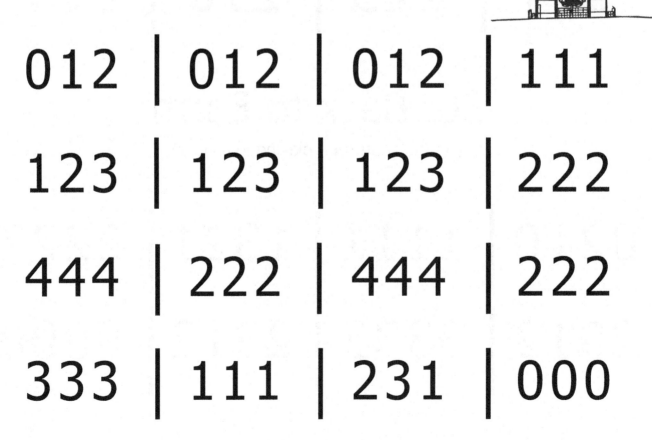

012 | 012 | 012 | 111

123 | 123 | 123 | 222

444 | 222 | 444 | 222

333 | 111 | 231 | 000

Reading Music

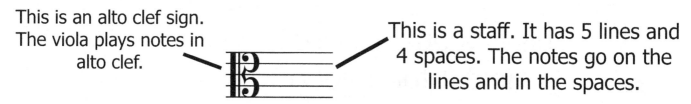

This is an alto clef sign. The viola plays notes in alto clef.

This is a staff. It has 5 lines and 4 spaces. The notes go on the lines and in the spaces.

The music notes are placed on the lines and in the spaces to mean certain sounds.

Space Notes
Every
Good
Boy
Deserves
Fudge

Line Notes
F
A
C
E
Guard

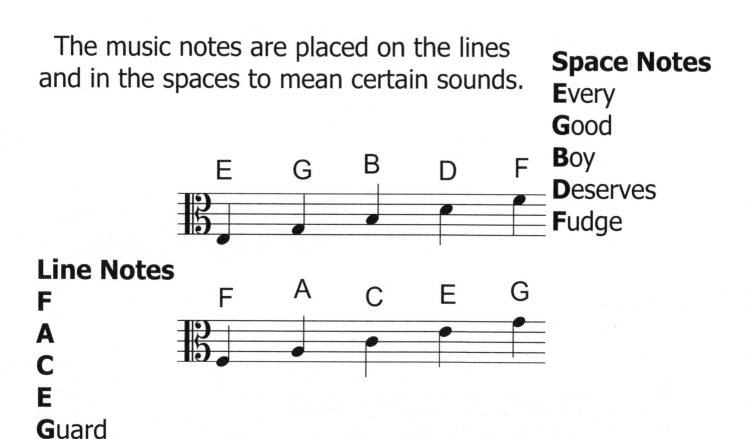

The notes go in order of the alphabet, from A to G, and then start back at A again.

34. Counting

This is a quarter note.
Hold it for 1 count.

This is a half note.
Hold it for 2 counts.

This is a whole note.
Hold it for 4 counts.

This is an eighth note.
Hold it for 1/2 a count.

 Two eighth notes
together equal
one quarter note (1 count.)

35. A and B on the A String

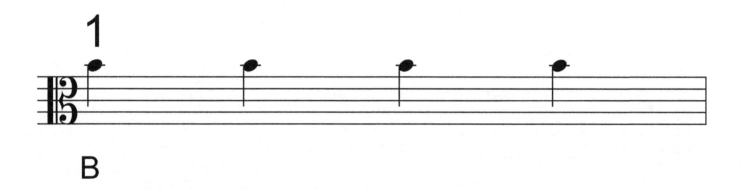

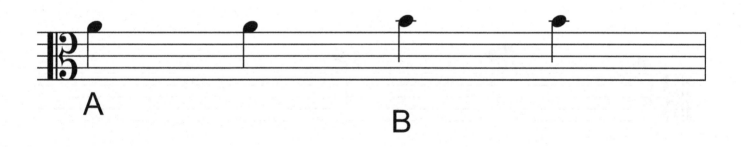

36. A, B, and C♯ on the A String

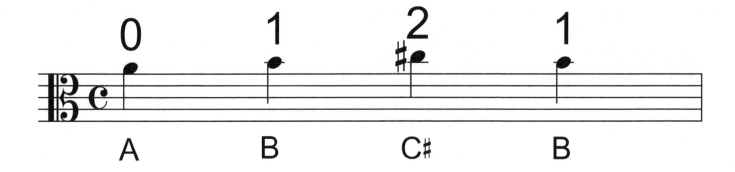

37. A, B, C♯, and D on the A String

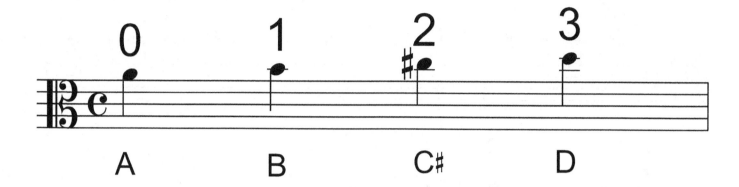

38. Boil Them Cabbage Down

39. Long-Short-Short Cabbage

40. ♩ Half Notes get 2 Counts

41. Mississippi Hot Dogs with Cabbage

42. Miss Mary Mack

43. D and E on the D String

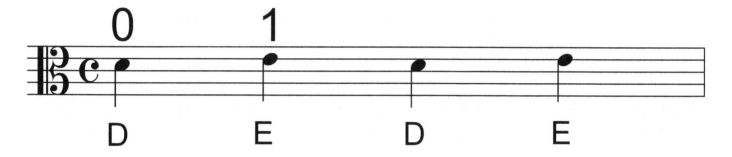

44. D, E, and F# on the D String

45. D, E, F♯, and G on the D String

46. Pickle Juice, Pickle Juice

47. Pickle Juice Stomp

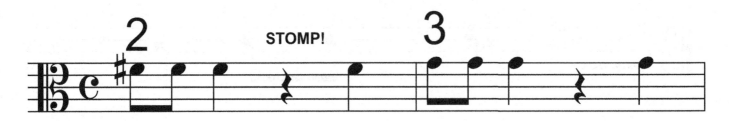

48. Peanut Butter Pie Pickle Juice

49. The Rattle Sna-wa-wake

50. The D string and the A string

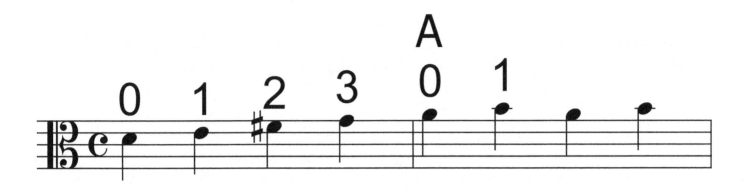

51. Playing on D and A

52. Who's That Knocking at my Window?

53. Pounding at the Window!

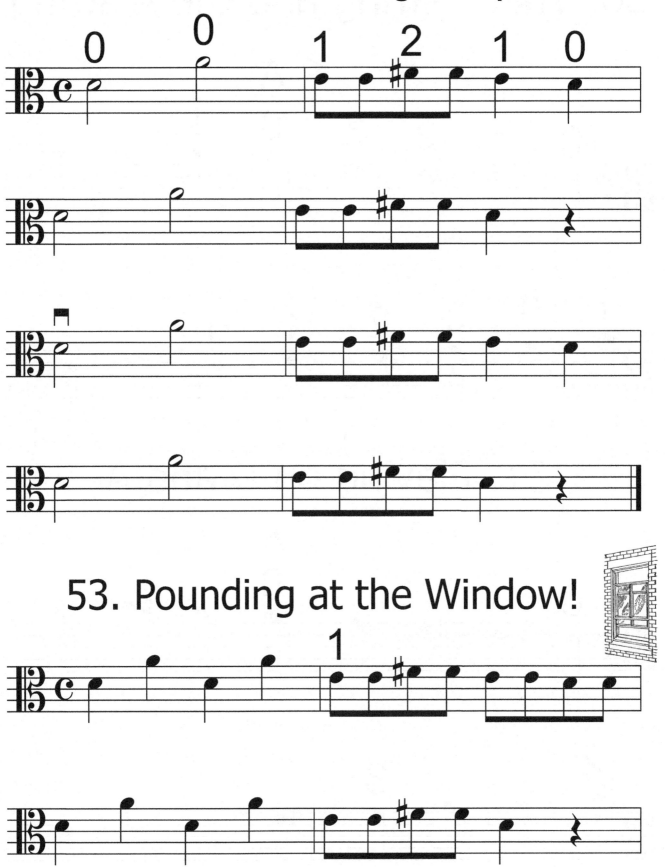

54. Tapping at the Window!

(Basses learn to shift to 3rd position here.)

55. The D Major Scale

56. Super Challenge!

57. Twinkle, Twinkle, Little Star

58. Twinkle, Twinkle (Mississippi Hot Dog)

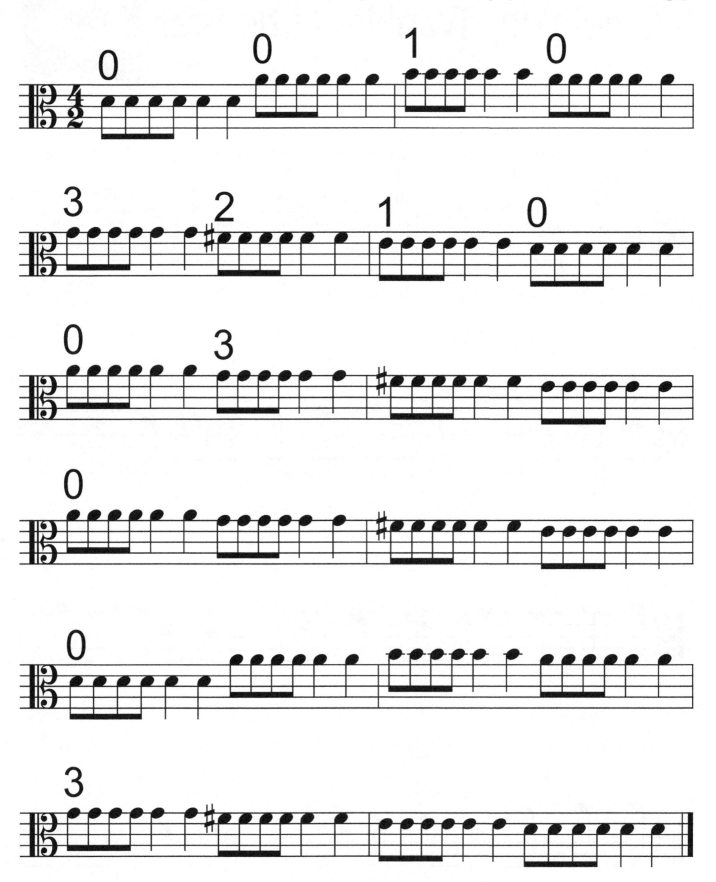

(Basses learn to shift to 3rd position here.)

59. Ode to Joy

Beethoven

First finger on the G string.

60. Fulton Had a Steamboat

61. Pickle Juice Steamboat

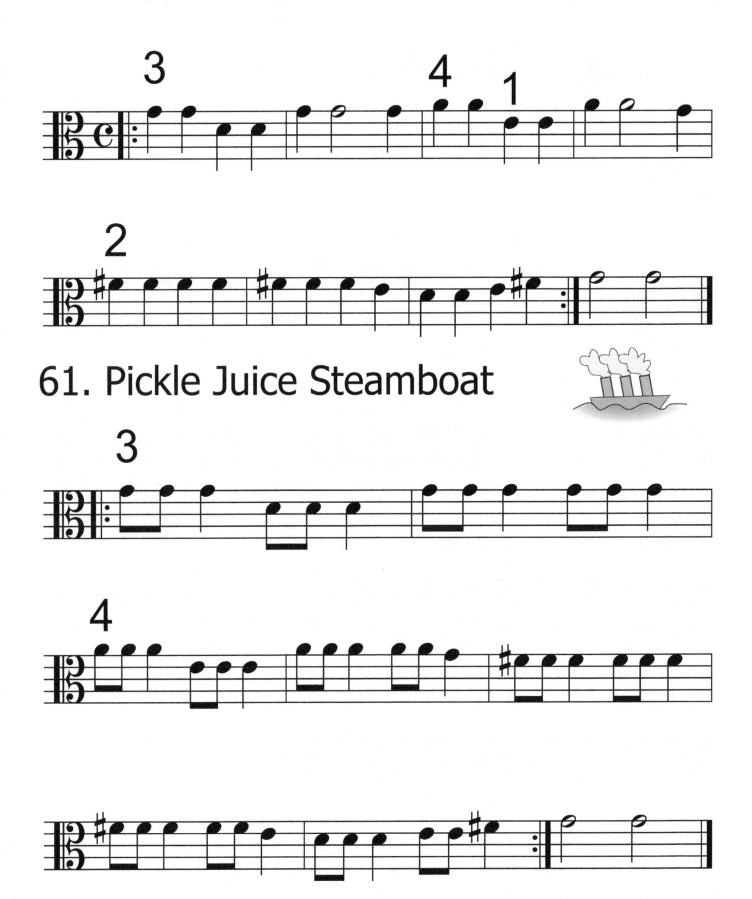

62. Blueberry Steamboat

63. Mississippi Hot Dog Steamboat

64. Jingle Bells

65. Dreidel Song

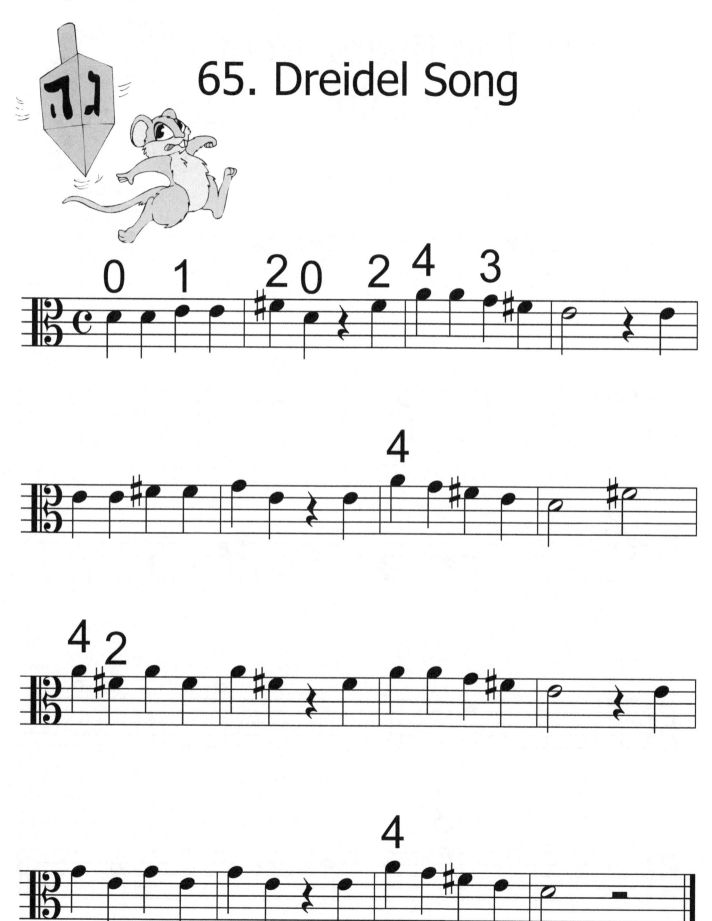

66. The Bears Went Over the Mountain

This note gets 3 counts.

67. Scotland's Burning: A Round

68. Old MacDonald

69. London Bridge

70. Cotton-Eyed Joe

71. Mississippi Hot Dog Joe

72. Blueberry Joe

73. Blueberry Pickle Juice Joe

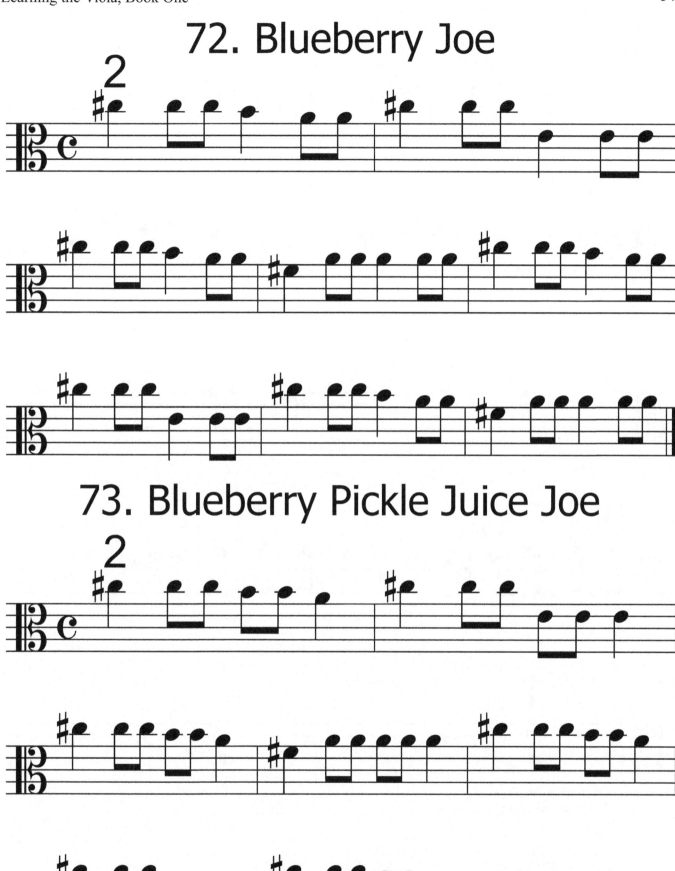

...

74. Frere Jacques

First finger on the G string.

75. Violins Learn E and F#

76. Violins Learn E, F#, and G#

77. Violins Learn E, F#, G#, and A

78. Violins Learn E, F#, G#, A, and B

79. The Grey Goose

80. A Goosey Variation

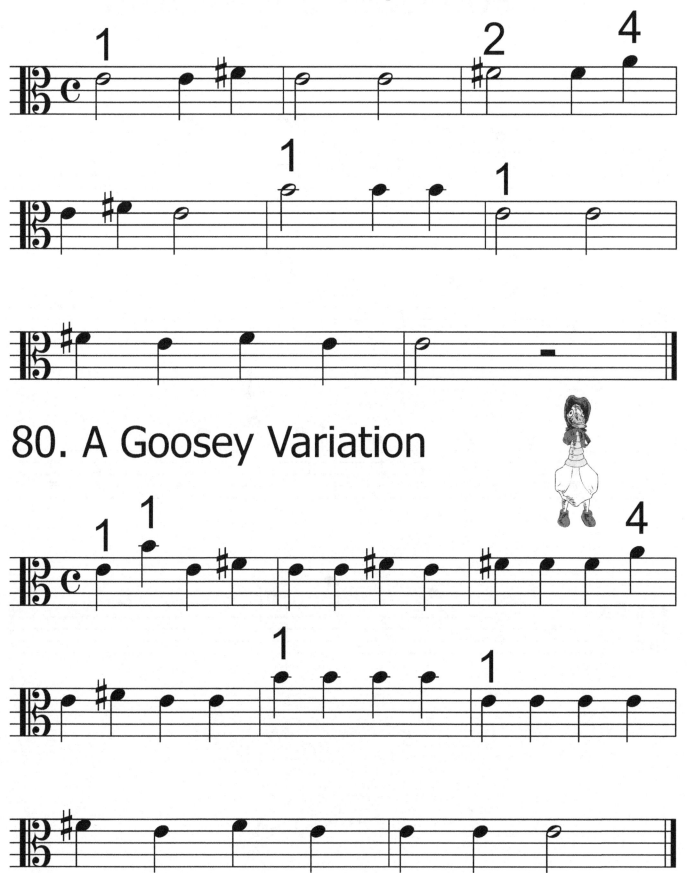

81. Pop Goes the Weasel

82. French Folk Song Harmony

83. French Folk Song

84. An Anonymous Allegro

85. G and A on the G String

0   1

G   A

86. G, A, and B on the G String

0   1   2

G   A   B

87. G, A, B, and C on the G String

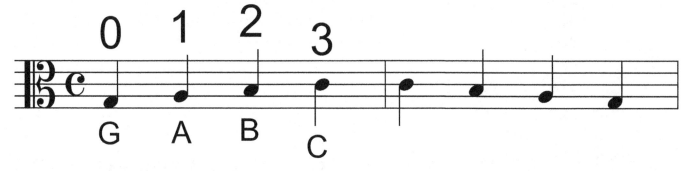

88. G, A, B, C, and D on the G String

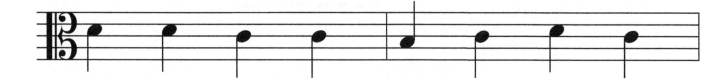

A-hunting we will go, a-hunting we will go
We'll catch a pig and dance a little jig
And then we'll let him go!

89. A-Hunting We Will Go

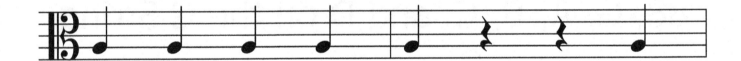

90. River Train

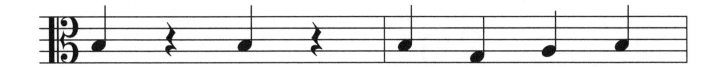

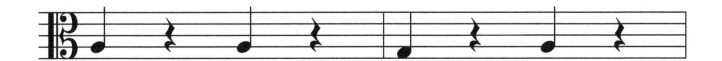

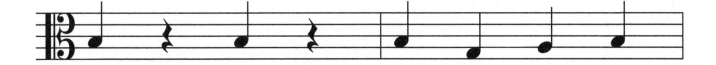

91. Dvorak's Largo

92. C and D on the C string

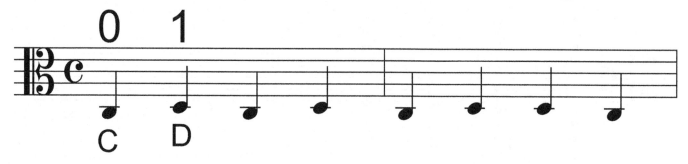

93. C, D, and E on the C string

94. C, D, E, and F on the C string

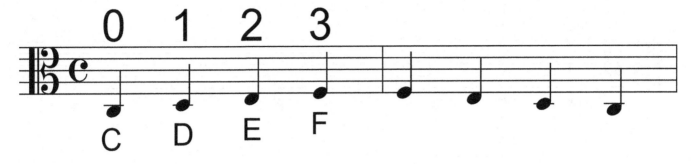

95. C, D, E, F, and G on the C string

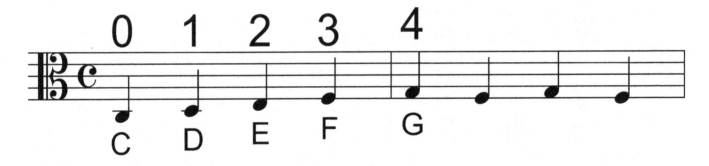

96. Hammer Ring

97. Won't You Ring, Old Hammer?

98. Yankee Doodle

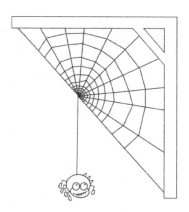

99. The Spider Song

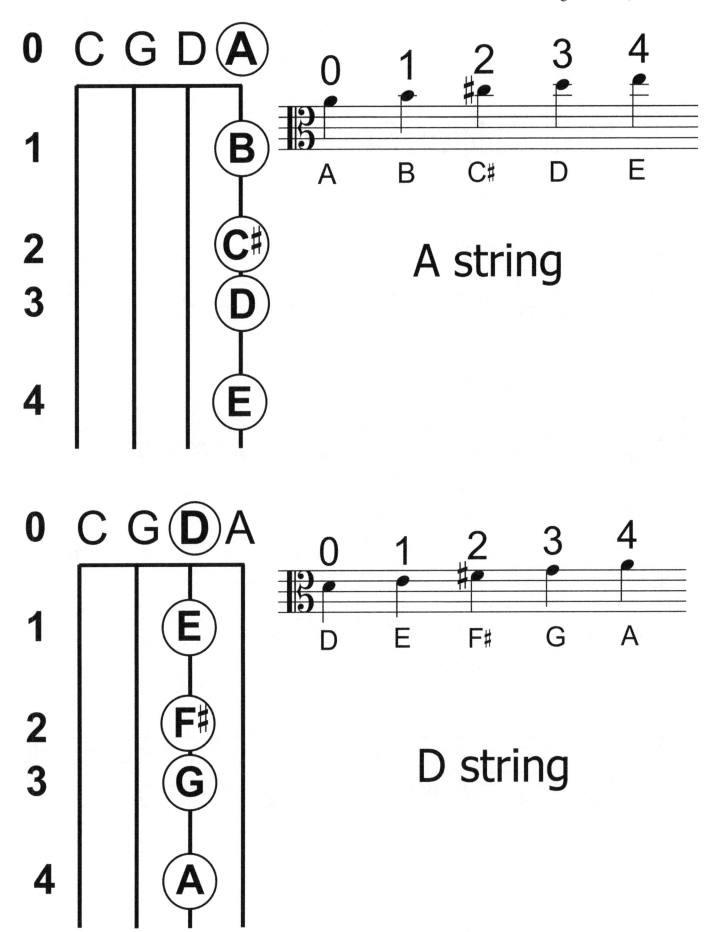

A string

D string

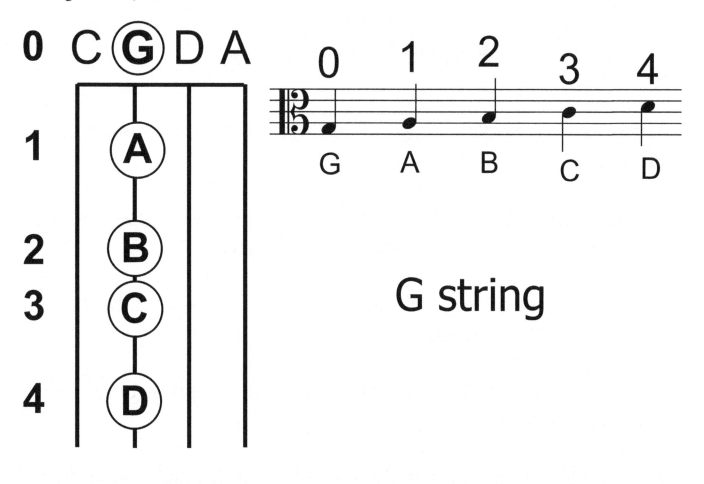

G string

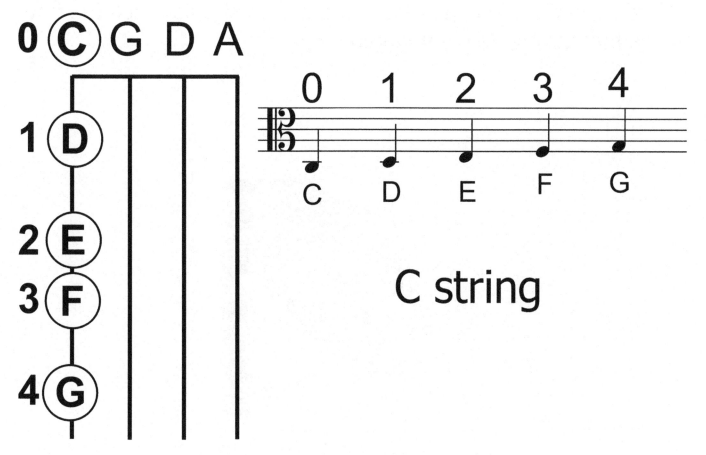

C string

How to Hold the Bow

1. The second (middle) finger covers the sideways "U" section of the frog.

2. The third (ring) finger covers the dot. If your bow does not have a dot, imagine a dot in the very center of the frog.

3. The fourth (pinky) fingertip rests gently on the top of the bow stick, with the finger lightly curved.

4. The first (index) finger rests on its side on the stick, between the first and second knuckles.

5. The thumb bends out slightly and rests on the stick, between the frog and the winding or grip. The thumb should touch the bow where the nail meets the fingertip.

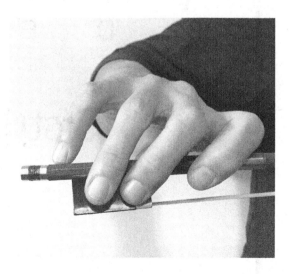

How to Hold the Bow

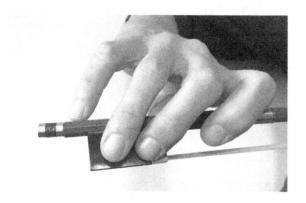

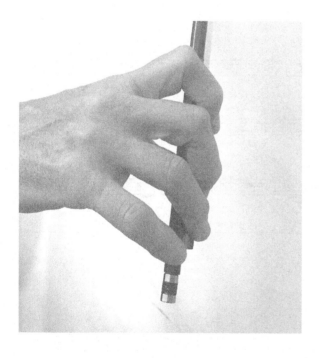

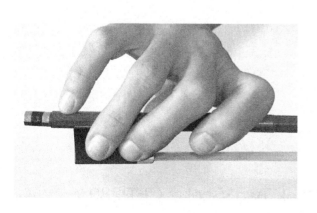

also available from www.charveypublications.com:

Learning the Viola, Book Two: CHP286

Can be used for
individual study, *single-string classes*,
or *mixed-string classes*, with:

Learning the Violin, Book Two: CHP285

Learning the Cello, Book Two: CHP287

Learning the Violin, Viola, Cello, and Bass, Book Two, Score: CHP289

also available from www.charveypublications.com

Playing the Viola, Book One: CHP299

Can be used for
individual study, *single-string classes*,
or *mixed-string classes*, with:

Playing the Violin, Book One: CHP298

Playing the Cello, Book One: CHP300

Playing the Bass, Book One: CHP301

Playing the Violin, Viola, Cello, and Bass, Book One, Score: CHP302

Made in the USA
Monee, IL
10 July 2020

36275268R00046

Learning the Viola, Book One: a number-to-reading method for individual lessons, single-string classes, or mixed-string classes!

available for
Violin: CHP280   Viola: CHP281
Cello: CHP282   Bass: CHP283
score/piano accompaniment available: CHP284

About this book

Learning the Viola, Book One is an introductory viola method for the absolute beginner. Starting with open string letters and songs with simple finger numbers, the book progresses to short exercises and familiar songs with large, easy-to-read notes to get the student to play as much as possible. Useful for all ages, *Learning the Viola, Book One* is especially helpful with younger beginners or students who struggle with note-reading. This book can be studied in private lessons, in single-string classes, or in mixed-string classes, along with *Learning the Violin, Book One, Learning the Cello, Book One*, and *Learning the Bass, Book One*. A score and piano accompaniment is also available. This book could be studied along with *The Open String Book for Viola* and could be followed by *Learning the Viola, Book Two*.

C. Harvey Publications
www.charveypublications.com

#CHP281
$8.95

ISBN 9780692542484

90000 >

9 780692 542484